This Motorcycle Log Book Belongs To:

____

____

____

Vehicle Information

Brand:	
Year:	
Make:	
Model:	
Engine:	
VIN Number:	
Vehicle Owner:	
Phone Number:	
Address:	
Purchase Date:	
Purchased From:	
Milage at Purchase:	
Plate Number:	
Insurance Comany:	
Agent:	
Signature:	

Monthly Maintenance Check   Year: _____________

	January	February	March	April	May	June	July	August	September	October	November	December
Battery												
Brakes/Fluid												
Spokes/Wheels												
Sprockets												
Fuel Filter												
Oil Level												
Chassis												
Coolant Level												
Air Filter												
Kickstand												
Hosepipe												
Lights												
Mileage												

Additional Notes: ____

____
____
____
____
____
____
____

Monthly Maintenance Check   Year:_________

	January	February	March	April	May	June	July	August	September	October	November	December
Battery												
Brakes/Fluid												
Spokes/Wheels												
Sprockets												
Fuel Filter												
Oil Level												
Chassis												
Coolant Level												
Air Filter												
Kickstand												
Hosepipe												
Lights												
Mileage												

Additional Notes:____

____

____

____

____

____

____

Monthly Maintenance Check   Year: ___________

	January	February	March	April	May	June	July	August	September	October	November	December
Battery												
Brakes/Fluid												
Spokes/Wheels												
Sprockets												
Fuel Filter												
Oil Level												
Chassis												
Coolant Level												
Air Filter												
Kickstand												
Hosepipe												
Lights												
Mileage												

Additional Notes: ____

____
____
____
____
____
____

Monthly Maintenance Check   Year: _____________

	January	February	March	April	May	June	July	August	September	October	November	December
Battery												
Brakes/Fluid												
Spokes/Wheels												
Sprockets												
Fuel Filter												
Oil Level												
Chassis												
Coolant Level												
Air Filter												
Kickstand												
Hosepipe												
Lights												
Mileage												

Additional Notes: ______________________________________

____

____

____

____

____

____

Monthly Maintenance Check   Year:________

	January	February	March	April	May	June	July	August	September	October	November	December
Battery												
Brakes/Fluid												
Spokes/Wheels												
Sprockets												
Fuel Filter												
Oil Level												
Chassis												
Coolant Level												
Air Filter												
Kickstand												
Hosepipe												
Lights												
Mileage												

Additional Notes:_______________________________

____
____
____
____
____
____

Monthly Maintenance Check   Year:_________

	January	February	March	April	May	June	July	August	September	October	November	December
Battery												
Brakes/Fluid												
Spokes/Wheels												
Sprockets												
Fuel Filter												
Oil Level												
Chassis												
Coolant Level												
Air Filter												
Kickstand												
Hosepipe												
Lights												
Mileage												

Additional Notes:____________________________________

____

____

____

____

____

____

Monthly Maintenance Check   Year:__________

	January	February	March	April	May	June	July	August	September	October	November	December
Battery												
Brakes/Fluid												
Spokes/Wheels												
Sprockets												
Fuel Filter												
Oil Level												
Chassis												
Coolant Level												
Air Filter												
Kickstand												
Hosepipe												
Lights												
Mileage												

Additional Notes:____

____
____
____
____
____
____

Monthly Maintenance Check   Year: __________

	January	February	March	April	May	June	July	August	September	October	November	December
Battery												
Brakes/Fluid												
Spokes/Wheels												
Sprockets												
Fuel Filter												
Oil Level												
Chassis												
Coolant Level												
Air Filter												
Kickstand												
Hosepipe												
Lights												
Mileage												

Additional Notes: _______________________________________

____

____

____

____

____

____

____

Monthly Maintenance Check   Year:__________

	January	February	March	April	May	June	July	August	September	October	November	December
Battery												
Brakes/Fluid												
Spokes/Wheels												
Sprockets												
Fuel Filter												
Oil Level												
Chassis												
Coolant Level												
Air Filter												
Kickstand												
Hosepipe												
Lights												
Mileage												

Additional Notes:____

____

____

____

____

____

____

Monthly Maintenance Check

Year:________

	January	February	March	April	May	June	July	August	September	October	November	December
Battery												
Brakes/Fluid												
Spokes/Wheels												
Sprockets												
Fuel Filter												
Oil Level												
Chassis												
Coolant Level												
Air Filter												
Kickstand												
Hosepipe												
Lights												
Mileage												

Additional Notes:_______________________________

____

____

____

____

____

____

Monthly Maintenance Check   Year:_________

	January	February	March	April	May	June	July	August	September	October	November	December
Battery												
Brakes/Fluid												
Spokes/Wheels												
Sprockets												
Fuel Filter												
Oil Level												
Chassis												
Coolant Level												
Air Filter												
Kickstand												
Hosepipe												
Lights												
Mileage												

Additional Notes:_________________________________

____
____
____
____
____
____
____

Monthly Maintenance Check

Year:__________

	January	February	March	April	May	June	July	August	September	October	November	December
Battery												
Brakes/Fluid												
Spokes/Wheels												
Sprockets												
Fuel Filter												
Oil Level												
Chassis												
Coolant Level												
Air Filter												
Kickstand												
Hosepipe												
Lights												
Mileage												

Additional Notes:______________________________________

____

____

____

____

____

____

Monthly Maintenance Check   Year:________

	January	February	March	April	May	June	July	August	September	October	November	December
Battery												
Brakes/Fluid												
Spokes/Wheels												
Sprockets												
Fuel Filter												
Oil Level												
Chassis												
Coolant Level												
Air Filter												
Kickstand												
Hosepipe												
Lights												
Mileage												

Additional Notes:______________________________________

____

____

____

____

____

____

Monthly Maintenance Check   Year:_________

	January	February	March	April	May	June	July	August	September	October	November	December
Battery												
Brakes/Fluid												
Spokes/Wheels												
Sprockets												
Fuel Filter												
Oil Level												
Chassis												
Coolant Level												
Air Filter												
Kickstand												
Hosepipe												
Lights												
Mileage												

Additional Notes:____

____

____

____

____

____

____

____

Monthly Maintenance Check

Year:_________

	January	February	March	April	May	June	July	August	September	October	November	December
Battery												
Brakes/Fluid												
Spokes/Wheels												
Sprockets												
Fuel Filter												
Oil Level												
Chassis												
Coolant Level												
Air Filter												
Kickstand												
Hosepipe												
Lights												
Mileage												

Additional Notes:_______________________________________

____
____
____
____
____
____
____

Monthly Maintenance Check   Year:___________

	January	February	March	April	May	June	July	August	September	October	November	December
Battery												
Brakes/Fluid												
Spokes/Wheels												
Sprockets												
Fuel Filter												
Oil Level												
Chassis												
Coolant Level												
Air Filter												
Kickstand												
Hosepipe												
Lights												
Mileage												

Additional Notes:_______________________________________

____

____

____

____

____

____

____

Monthly Maintenance Check   Year:________

	January	February	March	April	May	June	July	August	September	October	November	December
Battery												
Brakes/Fluid												
Spokes/Wheels												
Sprockets												
Fuel Filter												
Oil Level												
Chassis												
Coolant Level												
Air Filter												
Kickstand												
Hosepipe												
Lights												
Mileage												

Additional Notes:________________________________

____

____

____

____

____

____

Monthly Maintenance Check   Year:______________

	January	February	March	April	May	June	July	August	September	October	November	December
Battery												
Brakes/Fluid												
Spokes/Wheels												
Sprockets												
Fuel Filter												
Oil Level												
Chassis												
Coolant Level												
Air Filter												
Kickstand												
Hosepipe												
Lights												
Mileage												

Additional Notes:____

____

____

____

____

____

____

____

Monthly Maintenance Check

Year:_________

	January	February	March	April	May	June	July	August	September	October	November	December
Battery												
Brakes/Fluid												
Spokes/Wheels												
Sprockets												
Fuel Filter												
Oil Level												
Chassis												
Coolant Level												
Air Filter												
Kickstand												
Hosepipe												
Lights												
Mileage												

Additional Notes:______________________________________

____

____

____

____

____

____

____

Monthly Maintenance Check   Year:________

	January	February	March	April	May	June	July	August	September	October	November	December
Battery												
Brakes/Fluid												
Spokes/Wheels												
Sprockets												
Fuel Filter												
Oil Level												
Chassis												
Coolant Level												
Air Filter												
Kickstand												
Hosepipe												
Lights												
Mileage												

Additional Notes:____

____

____

____

____

____

____

Monthly Maintenance Check   Year:_________

	January	February	March	April	May	June	July	August	September	October	November	December
Battery												
Brakes/Fluid												
Spokes/Wheels												
Sprockets												
Fuel Filter												
Oil Level												
Chassis												
Coolant Level												
Air Filter												
Kickstand												
Hosepipe												
Lights												
Mileage												

Additional Notes:_____________________________________

____

____

____

____

____

____

Monthly Maintenance Check   Year:_____________

	January	February	March	April	May	June	July	August	September	October	November	December
Battery												
Brakes/Fluid												
Spokes/Wheels												
Sprockets												
Fuel Filter												
Oil Level												
Chassis												
Coolant Level												
Air Filter												
Kickstand												
Hosepipe												
Lights												
Mileage												

Additional Notes:____

____
____
____
____
____
____
____

Monthly Maintenance Check   Year: ________

	January	February	March	April	May	June	July	August	September	October	November	December
Battery												
Brakes/Fluid												
Spokes/Wheels												
Sprockets												
Fuel Filter												
Oil Level												
Chassis												
Coolant Level												
Air Filter												
Kickstand												
Hosepipe												
Lights												
Mileage												

Additional Notes: ____

____

____

____

____

____

____

Monthly Maintenance Check   Year:_________

	January	February	March	April	May	June	July	August	September	October	November	December
Battery												
Brakes/Fluid												
Spokes/Wheels												
Sprockets												
Fuel Filter												
Oil Level												
Chassis												
Coolant Level												
Air Filter												
Kickstand												
Hosepipe												
Lights												
Mileage												

Additional Notes:____

____

____

____

____

____

____

Monthly Maintenance Check   Year:___________

	January	February	March	April	May	June	July	August	September	October	November	December
Battery												
Brakes/Fluid												
Spokes/Wheels												
Sprockets												
Fuel Filter												
Oil Level												
Chassis												
Coolant Level												
Air Filter												
Kickstand												
Hosepipe												
Lights												
Mileage												

Additional Notes:_______________________________________

____
____
____
____
____
____
____

Monthly Maintenance Check   Year:_____________

	January	February	March	April	May	June	July	August	September	October	November	December
Battery												
Brakes/Fluid												
Spokes/Wheels												
Sprockets												
Fuel Filter												
Oil Level												
Chassis												
Coolant Level												
Air Filter												
Kickstand												
Hosepipe												
Lights												
Mileage												

Additional Notes:____

____

____

____

____

____

____

____

Monthly Maintenance Check   Year:__________

	January	February	March	April	May	June	July	August	September	October	November	December
Battery												
Brakes/Fluid												
Spokes/Wheels												
Sprockets												
Fuel Filter												
Oil Level												
Chassis												
Coolant Level												
Air Filter												
Kickstand												
Hosepipe												
Lights												
Mileage												

Additional Notes:______________________________________

____

____

____

____

____

____

____

Monthly Maintenance Check   Year:______________

	January	February	March	April	May	June	July	August	September	October	November	December
Battery												
Brakes/Fluid												
Spokes/Wheels												
Sprockets												
Fuel Filter												
Oil Level												
Chassis												
Coolant Level												
Air Filter												
Kickstand												
Hosepipe												
Lights												
Mileage												

Additional Notes:____

____

____

____

____

____

____

____

Monthly Maintenance Check   Year: _________

	January	February	March	April	May	June	July	August	September	October	November	December
Battery												
Brakes/Fluid												
Spokes/Wheels												
Sprockets												
Fuel Filter												
Oil Level												
Chassis												
Coolant Level												
Air Filter												
Kickstand												
Hosepipe												
Lights												
Mileage												

Additional Notes:____

____

____

____

____

____

____

____

Monthly Maintenance Check   Year:_________

	January	February	March	April	May	June	July	August	September	October	November	December
Battery												
Brakes/Fluid												
Spokes/Wheels												
Sprockets												
Fuel Filter												
Oil Level												
Chassis												
Coolant Level												
Air Filter												
Kickstand												
Hosepipe												
Lights												
Mileage												

Additional Notes:_______________________________________

____
____
____
____
____
____
____

Monthly Maintenance Check   Year:________

	January	February	March	April	May	June	July	August	September	October	November	December
Battery												
Brakes/Fluid												
Spokes/Wheels												
Sprockets												
Fuel Filter												
Oil Level												
Chassis												
Coolant Level												
Air Filter												
Kickstand												
Hosepipe												
Lights												
Mileage												

Additional Notes:____________________________________

____

____

____

____

____

____

____

Monthly Maintenance Check

Year: _____________

	January	February	March	April	May	June	July	August	September	October	November	December
Battery												
Brakes/Fluid												
Spokes/Wheels												
Sprockets												
Fuel Filter												
Oil Level												
Chassis												
Coolant Level												
Air Filter												
Kickstand												
Hosepipe												
Lights												
Mileage												

Additional Notes: ____

____

____

____

____

____

____

____

Vehicle Information

Brand:	
Year:	
Make:	
Model:	
Engine:	
VIN Number:	
Vehicle Owner:	
Phone Number:	
Address:	
Purchase Date:	
Purchased From:	
Milage at Purchase:	
Plate Number:	
Insurance Comany:	
Agent:	
Signature:	

Monthly Maintenance Check   Year:_________

	January	February	March	April	May	June	July	August	September	October	November	December
Battery												
Brakes/Fluid												
Spokes/Wheels												
Sprockets												
Fuel Filter												
Oil Level												
Chassis												
Coolant Level												
Air Filter												
Kickstand												
Hosepipe												
Lights												
Mileage												

Additional Notes:____

____

____

____

____

____

____

Monthly Maintenance Check   Year:________

	January	February	March	April	May	June	July	August	September	October	November	December
Battery												
Brakes/Fluid												
Spokes/Wheels												
Sprockets												
Fuel Filter												
Oil Level												
Chassis												
Coolant Level												
Air Filter												
Kickstand												
Hosepipe												
Lights												
Mileage												

Additional Notes:________________________________

____

____

____

____

____

____

Monthly Maintenance Check   Year:_________

	January	February	March	April	May	June	July	August	September	October	November	December
Battery												
Brakes/Fluid												
Spokes/Wheels												
Sprockets												
Fuel Filter												
Oil Level												
Chassis												
Coolant Level												
Air Filter												
Kickstand												
Hosepipe												
Lights												
Mileage												

Additional Notes:____

____

____

____

____

____

____

Monthly Maintenance Check   Year:_________

	January	February	March	April	May	June	July	August	September	October	November	December
Battery												
Brakes/Fluid												
Spokes/Wheels												
Sprockets												
Fuel Filter												
Oil Level												
Chassis												
Coolant Level												
Air Filter												
Kickstand												
Hosepipe												
Lights												
Mileage												

Additional Notes:_______________________________________

____

____

____

____

____

____

Monthly Maintenance Check   Year:_________

	January	February	March	April	May	June	July	August	September	October	November	December
Battery												
Brakes/Fluid												
Spokes/Wheels												
Sprockets												
Fuel Filter												
Oil Level												
Chassis												
Coolant Level												
Air Filter												
Kickstand												
Hosepipe												
Lights												
Mileage												

Additional Notes:_________________________________

____
____
____
____
____
____
____

Monthly Maintenance Check   Year:__________

	January	February	March	April	May	June	July	August	September	October	November	December
Battery												
Brakes/Fluid												
Spokes/Wheels												
Sprockets												
Fuel Filter												
Oil Level												
Chassis												
Coolant Level												
Air Filter												
Kickstand												
Hosepipe												
Lights												
Mileage												

Additional Notes:_______________________________________

____
____
____
____
____
____
____

Monthly Maintenance Check   Year:________

	January	February	March	April	May	June	July	August	September	October	November	December
Battery												
Brakes/Fluid												
Spokes/Wheels												
Sprockets												
Fuel Filter												
Oil Level												
Chassis												
Coolant Level												
Air Filter												
Kickstand												
Hosepipe												
Lights												
Mileage												

Additional Notes:____

____

____

____

____

____

____

____

Monthly Maintenance Check   Year:______

	January	February	March	April	May	June	July	August	September	October	November	December
Battery												
Brakes/Fluid												
Spokes/Wheels												
Sprockets												
Fuel Filter												
Oil Level												
Chassis												
Coolant Level												
Air Filter												
Kickstand												
Hosepipe												
Lights												
Mileage												

Additional Notes:_______________________________

____
____
____
____
____
____
____

Monthly Maintenance Check

Year:________

	January	February	March	April	May	June	July	August	September	October	November	December
Battery												
Brakes/Fluid												
Spokes/Wheels												
Sprockets												
Fuel Filter												
Oil Level												
Chassis												
Coolant Level												
Air Filter												
Kickstand												
Hosepipe												
Lights												
Mileage												

Additional Notes:____________________________________

____

____

____

____

____

____

____

Monthly Maintenance Check   Year:__________

	January	February	March	April	May	June	July	August	September	October	November	December
Battery												
Brakes/Fluid												
Spokes/Wheels												
Sprockets												
Fuel Filter												
Oil Level												
Chassis												
Coolant Level												
Air Filter												
Kickstand												
Hosepipe												
Lights												
Mileage												

Additional Notes:____

____
____
____
____
____
____
____

Monthly Maintenance Check   Year:_______

	January	February	March	April	May	June	July	August	September	October	November	December
Battery												
Brakes/Fluid												
Spokes/Wheels												
Sprockets												
Fuel Filter												
Oil Level												
Chassis												
Coolant Level												
Air Filter												
Kickstand												
Hosepipe												
Lights												
Mileage												

Additional Notes:_______________________________________

____
____
____
____
____
____

Monthly Maintenance Check   Year:_________

	January	February	March	April	May	June	July	August	September	October	November	December
Battery												
Brakes/Fluid												
Spokes/Wheels												
Sprockets												
Fuel Filter												
Oil Level												
Chassis												
Coolant Level												
Air Filter												
Kickstand												
Hosepipe												
Lights												
Mileage												

Additional Notes:______________________________________

____

____

____

____

____

____

Monthly Maintenance Check

Year: ___________

	January	February	March	April	May	June	July	August	September	October	November	December
Battery												
Brakes/Fluid												
Spokes/Wheels												
Sprockets												
Fuel Filter												
Oil Level												
Chassis												
Coolant Level												
Air Filter												
Kickstand												
Hosepipe												
Lights												
Mileage												

Additional Notes: ______________________________________

____

____

____

____

____

____

____

Monthly Maintenance Check   Year: _________

	January	February	March	April	May	June	July	August	September	October	November	December
Battery												
Brakes/Fluid												
Spokes/Wheels												
Sprockets												
Fuel Filter												
Oil Level												
Chassis												
Coolant Level												
Air Filter												
Kickstand												
Hosepipe												
Lights												
Mileage												

Additional Notes: ____

____

____

____

____

____

____

____

Monthly Maintenance Check

Year:_________

	January	February	March	April	May	June	July	August	September	October	November	December
Battery												
Brakes/Fluid												
Spokes/Wheels												
Sprockets												
Fuel Filter												
Oil Level												
Chassis												
Coolant Level												
Air Filter												
Kickstand												
Hosepipe												
Lights												
Mileage												

Additional Notes:__________________________________

____

____

____

____

____

____

Monthly Maintenance Check   Year:_________

	January	February	March	April	May	June	July	August	September	October	November	December
Battery												
Brakes/Fluid												
Spokes/Wheels												
Sprockets												
Fuel Filter												
Oil Level												
Chassis												
Coolant Level												
Air Filter												
Kickstand												
Hosepipe												
Lights												
Mileage												

Additional Notes:_______________________________

____
____
____
____
____
____

Monthly Maintenance Check   Year:____________

	January	February	March	April	May	June	July	August	September	October	November	December
Battery												
Brakes/Fluid												
Spokes/Wheels												
Sprockets												
Fuel Filter												
Oil Level												
Chassis												
Coolant Level												
Air Filter												
Kickstand												
Hosepipe												
Lights												
Mileage												

Additional Notes:____

____

____

____

____

____

____

____

Monthly Maintenance Check   Year:________

	January	February	March	April	May	June	July	August	September	October	November	December
Battery												
Brakes/Fluid												
Spokes/Wheels												
Sprockets												
Fuel Filter												
Oil Level												
Chassis												
Coolant Level												
Air Filter												
Kickstand												
Hosepipe												
Lights												
Mileage												

Additional Notes:____

____
____
____
____
____
____

Monthly Maintenance Check   Year:_____________

	January	February	March	April	May	June	July	August	September	October	November	December
Battery												
Brakes/Fluid												
Spokes/Wheels												
Sprockets												
Fuel Filter												
Oil Level												
Chassis												
Coolant Level												
Air Filter												
Kickstand												
Hosepipe												
Lights												
Mileage												

Additional Notes:_______________________________________

____

____

____

____

____

____

____

Monthly Maintenance Check   Year: _________

	January	February	March	April	May	June	July	August	September	October	November	December
Battery												
Brakes/Fluid												
Spokes/Wheels												
Sprockets												
Fuel Filter												
Oil Level												
Chassis												
Coolant Level												
Air Filter												
Kickstand												
Hosepipe												
Lights												
Mileage												

Additional Notes: _______________________________________

____

____

____

____

____

____

Monthly Maintenance Check

Year:________

	January	February	March	April	May	June	July	August	September	October	November	December
Battery												
Brakes/Fluid												
Spokes/Wheels												
Sprockets												
Fuel Filter												
Oil Level												
Chassis												
Coolant Level												
Air Filter												
Kickstand												
Hosepipe												
Lights												
Mileage												

Additional Notes:____

____

____

____

____

____

____

Monthly Maintenance Check   Year: __________

	January	February	March	April	May	June	July	August	September	October	November	December
Battery												
Brakes/Fluid												
Spokes/Wheels												
Sprockets												
Fuel Filter												
Oil Level												
Chassis												
Coolant Level												
Air Filter												
Kickstand												
Hosepipe												
Lights												
Mileage												

Additional Notes: _______________________________________

____
____
____
____
____
____
____

Monthly Maintenance Check

Year:_____________

	January	February	March	April	May	June	July	August	September	October	November	December
Battery												
Brakes/Fluid												
Spokes/Wheels												
Sprockets												
Fuel Filter												
Oil Level												
Chassis												
Coolant Level												
Air Filter												
Kickstand												
Hosepipe												
Lights												
Mileage												

Additional Notes:____

____

____

____

____

____

____

Monthly Maintenance Check   Year: _______________

	January	February	March	April	May	June	July	August	September	October	November	December
Battery												
Brakes/Fluid												
Spokes/Wheels												
Sprockets												
Fuel Filter												
Oil Level												
Chassis												
Coolant Level												
Air Filter												
Kickstand												
Hosepipe												
Lights												
Mileage												

Additional Notes: _______________________________________

____

____

____

____

____

____

Monthly Maintenance Check

Year:__________

	January	February	March	April	May	June	July	August	September	October	November	December
Battery												
Brakes/Fluid												
Spokes/Wheels												
Sprockets												
Fuel Filter												
Oil Level												
Chassis												
Coolant Level												
Air Filter												
Kickstand												
Hosepipe												
Lights												
Mileage												

Additional Notes:___________________________

____

____

____

____

____

____

Monthly Maintenance Check   Year:＿＿＿＿＿＿

	January	February	March	April	May	June	July	August	September	October	November	December
Battery												
Brakes/Fluid												
Spokes/Wheels												
Sprockets												
Fuel Filter												
Oil Level												
Chassis												
Coolant Level												
Air Filter												
Kickstand												
Hosepipe												
Lights												
Mileage												

Additional Notes:＿＿＿＿＿＿＿＿＿＿＿＿＿＿＿＿＿＿＿＿＿＿＿＿＿＿＿＿＿＿＿＿

＿＿＿

＿＿＿

＿＿＿

＿＿＿

＿＿＿

＿＿＿

Monthly Maintenance Check   Year:_________

	January	February	March	April	May	June	July	August	September	October	November	December
Battery												
Brakes/Fluid												
Spokes/Wheels												
Sprockets												
Fuel Filter												
Oil Level												
Chassis												
Coolant Level												
Air Filter												
Kickstand												
Hosepipe												
Lights												
Mileage												

Additional Notes:____

____

____

____

____

____

____

____

Monthly Maintenance Check   Year:______________

	January	February	March	April	May	June	July	August	September	October	November	December
Battery												
Brakes/Fluid												
Spokes/Wheels												
Sprockets												
Fuel Filter												
Oil Level												
Chassis												
Coolant Level												
Air Filter												
Kickstand												
Hosepipe												
Lights												
Mileage												

Additional Notes:____

____

____

____

____

____

____

____

Monthly Maintenance Check

Year:__________

	January	February	March	April	May	June	July	August	September	October	November	December
Battery												
Brakes/Fluid												
Spokes/Wheels												
Sprockets												
Fuel Filter												
Oil Level												
Chassis												
Coolant Level												
Air Filter												
Kickstand												
Hosepipe												
Lights												
Mileage												

Additional Notes:__________________________________

____

____

____

____

____

____

Monthly Maintenance Check   Year:_________

	January	February	March	April	May	June	July	August	September	October	November	December
Battery												
Brakes/Fluid												
Spokes/Wheels												
Sprockets												
Fuel Filter												
Oil Level												
Chassis												
Coolant Level												
Air Filter												
Kickstand												
Hosepipe												
Lights												
Mileage												

Additional Notes:________________________________

____
____
____
____
____
____
____

Monthly Maintenance Check   Year:_____________

	January	February	March	April	May	June	July	August	September	October	November	December
Battery												
Brakes/Fluid												
Spokes/Wheels												
Sprockets												
Fuel Filter												
Oil Level												
Chassis												
Coolant Level												
Air Filter												
Kickstand												
Hosepipe												
Lights												
Mileage												

Additional Notes:____

____

____

____

____

____

____

____

____

Monthly Maintenance Check

Year: _______________

	January	February	March	April	May	June	July	August	September	October	November	December
Battery												
Brakes/Fluid												
Spokes/Wheels												
Sprockets												
Fuel Filter												
Oil Level												
Chassis												
Coolant Level												
Air Filter												
Kickstand												
Hosepipe												
Lights												
Mileage												

Additional Notes: ____

____
____
____
____
____
____

Vehicle Information

Brand:	
Year:	
Make:	
Model:	
Engine:	
VIN Number:	
Vehicle Owner:	
Phone Number:	
Address:	
Purchase Date:	
Purchased From:	
Milage at Purchase:	
Plate Number:	
Insurance Comany:	
Agent:	
Signature:	

Monthly Maintenance Check Year:______________

	January	February	March	April	May	June	July	August	September	October	November	December
Battery												
Brakes/Fluid												
Spokes/Wheels												
Sprockets												
Fuel Filter												
Oil Level												
Chassis												
Coolant Level												
Air Filter												
Kickstand												
Hosepipe												
Lights												
Mileage												

Additional Notes:____

____

____

____

____

____

____

Monthly Maintenance Check   Year:_________

	January	February	March	April	May	June	July	August	September	October	November	December
Battery												
Brakes/Fluid												
Spokes/Wheels												
Sprockets												
Fuel Filter												
Oil Level												
Chassis												
Coolant Level												
Air Filter												
Kickstand												
Hosepipe												
Lights												
Mileage												

Additional Notes:____

____

____

____

____

____

____

Monthly Maintenance Check   Year:__________

	January	February	March	April	May	June	July	August	September	October	November	December
Battery												
Brakes/Fluid												
Spokes/Wheels												
Sprockets												
Fuel Filter												
Oil Level												
Chassis												
Coolant Level												
Air Filter												
Kickstand												
Hosepipe												
Lights												
Mileage												

Additional Notes:____

____

____

____

____

____

____

Monthly Maintenance Check   Year:_________

	January	February	March	April	May	June	July	August	September	October	November	December
Battery												
Brakes/Fluid												
Spokes/Wheels												
Sprockets												
Fuel Filter												
Oil Level												
Chassis												
Coolant Level												
Air Filter												
Kickstand												
Hosepipe												
Lights												
Mileage												

Additional Notes:____

____
____
____
____
____
____
____

Monthly Maintenance Check   Year:________

	January	February	March	April	May	June	July	August	September	October	November	December
Battery												
Brakes/Fluid												
Spokes/Wheels												
Sprockets												
Fuel Filter												
Oil Level												
Chassis												
Coolant Level												
Air Filter												
Kickstand												
Hosepipe												
Lights												
Mileage												

Additional Notes:________________________________

____
____
____
____
____
____
____

Monthly Maintenance Check   Year:__________

	January	February	March	April	May	June	July	August	September	October	November	December
Battery												
Brakes/Fluid												
Spokes/Wheels												
Sprockets												
Fuel Filter												
Oil Level												
Chassis												
Coolant Level												
Air Filter												
Kickstand												
Hosepipe												
Lights												
Mileage												

Additional Notes:____

____

____

____

____

____

____

____

Monthly Maintenance Check   Year:________

	January	February	March	April	May	June	July	August	September	October	November	December
Battery												
Brakes/Fluid												
Spokes/Wheels												
Sprockets												
Fuel Filter												
Oil Level												
Chassis												
Coolant Level												
Air Filter												
Kickstand												
Hosepipe												
Lights												
Mileage												

Additional Notes:____

____

____

____

____

____

____

Monthly Maintenance Check

Year:__________

	January	February	March	April	May	June	July	August	September	October	November	December
Battery												
Brakes/Fluid												
Spokes/Wheels												
Sprockets												
Fuel Filter												
Oil Level												
Chassis												
Coolant Level												
Air Filter												
Kickstand												
Hosepipe												
Lights												
Mileage												

Additional Notes:_____________________________________

____

____

____

____

____

____

Monthly Maintenance Check   Year:________

	January	February	March	April	May	June	July	August	September	October	November	December
Battery												
Brakes/Fluid												
Spokes/Wheels												
Sprockets												
Fuel Filter												
Oil Level												
Chassis												
Coolant Level												
Air Filter												
Kickstand												
Hosepipe												
Lights												
Mileage												

Additional Notes:_________________________________

____

____

____

____

____

____

Monthly Maintenance Check   Year: _____________

	January	February	March	April	May	June	July	August	September	October	November	December
Battery												
Brakes/Fluid												
Spokes/Wheels												
Sprockets												
Fuel Filter												
Oil Level												
Chassis												
Coolant Level												
Air Filter												
Kickstand												
Hosepipe												
Lights												
Mileage												

Additional Notes: _______________________________________

____

____

____

____

____

____

Monthly Maintenance Check   Year: _________

	January	February	March	April	May	June	July	August	September	October	November	December
Battery												
Brakes/Fluid												
Spokes/Wheels												
Sprockets												
Fuel Filter												
Oil Level												
Chassis												
Coolant Level												
Air Filter												
Kickstand												
Hosepipe												
Lights												
Mileage												

Additional Notes: _______________________________________

____

____

____

____

____

____

____

Monthly Maintenance Check   Year:_________

	January	February	March	April	May	June	July	August	September	October	November	December
Battery												
Brakes/Fluid												
Spokes/Wheels												
Sprockets												
Fuel Filter												
Oil Level												
Chassis												
Coolant Level												
Air Filter												
Kickstand												
Hosepipe												
Lights												
Mileage												

Additional Notes:____

____

____

____

____

____

____

____

Monthly Maintenance Check   Year:______

	January	February	March	April	May	June	July	August	September	October	November	December
Battery												
Brakes/Fluid												
Spokes/Wheels												
Sprockets												
Fuel Filter												
Oil Level												
Chassis												
Coolant Level												
Air Filter												
Kickstand												
Hosepipe												
Lights												
Mileage												

Additional Notes:___________________________________

____
____
____
____
____
____

Monthly Maintenance Check   Year: _____________

	January	February	March	April	May	June	July	August	September	October	November	December
Battery												
Brakes/Fluid												
Spokes/Wheels												
Sprockets												
Fuel Filter												
Oil Level												
Chassis												
Coolant Level												
Air Filter												
Kickstand												
Hosepipe												
Lights												
Mileage												

Additional Notes: _______________________________________

____
____
____
____
____
____
____

Monthly Maintenance Check   Year:_________

	January	February	March	April	May	June	July	August	September	October	November	December
Battery												
Brakes/Fluid												
Spokes/Wheels												
Sprockets												
Fuel Filter												
Oil Level												
Chassis												
Coolant Level												
Air Filter												
Kickstand												
Hosepipe												
Lights												
Mileage												

Additional Notes:____

____
____
____
____
____
____

Monthly Maintenance Check   Year:_________

	January	February	March	April	May	June	July	August	September	October	November	December
Battery												
Brakes/Fluid												
Spokes/Wheels												
Sprockets												
Fuel Filter												
Oil Level												
Chassis												
Coolant Level												
Air Filter												
Kickstand												
Hosepipe												
Lights												
Mileage												

Additional Notes:_______________________________________

____

____

____

____

____

____

Monthly Maintenance Check   Year:________

	January	February	March	April	May	June	July	August	September	October	November	December
Battery												
Brakes/Fluid												
Spokes/Wheels												
Sprockets												
Fuel Filter												
Oil Level												
Chassis												
Coolant Level												
Air Filter												
Kickstand												
Hosepipe												
Lights												
Mileage												

Additional Notes:____

____

____

____

____

____

____

Monthly Maintenance Check   Year:__________

	January	February	March	April	May	June	July	August	September	October	November	December
Battery												
Brakes/Fluid												
Spokes/Wheels												
Sprockets												
Fuel Filter												
Oil Level												
Chassis												
Coolant Level												
Air Filter												
Kickstand												
Hosepipe												
Lights												
Mileage												

Additional Notes:____

____

____

____

____

____

____

____

Monthly Maintenance Check   Year:__________

	January	February	March	April	May	June	July	August	September	October	November	December
Battery												
Brakes/Fluid												
Spokes/Wheels												
Sprockets												
Fuel Filter												
Oil Level												
Chassis												
Coolant Level												
Air Filter												
Kickstand												
Hosepipe												
Lights												
Mileage												

Additional Notes:________________________________

____

____

____

____

____

____

Monthly Maintenance Check   Year:_________

	January	February	March	April	May	June	July	August	September	October	November	December
Battery												
Brakes/Fluid												
Spokes/Wheels												
Sprockets												
Fuel Filter												
Oil Level												
Chassis												
Coolant Level												
Air Filter												
Kickstand												
Hosepipe												
Lights												
Mileage												

Additional Notes:____

____
____
____
____
____
____
____

Monthly Maintenance Check   Year:__________

	January	February	March	April	May	June	July	August	September	October	November	December
Battery												
Brakes/Fluid												
Spokes/Wheels												
Sprockets												
Fuel Filter												
Oil Level												
Chassis												
Coolant Level												
Air Filter												
Kickstand												
Hosepipe												
Lights												
Mileage												

Additional Notes:____

____

____

____

____

____

____

____

Monthly Maintenance Check   Year:______

	January	February	March	April	May	June	July	August	September	October	November	December
Battery												
Brakes/Fluid												
Spokes/Wheels												
Sprockets												
Fuel Filter												
Oil Level												
Chassis												
Coolant Level												
Air Filter												
Kickstand												
Hosepipe												
Lights												
Mileage												

Additional Notes:______________________________________

____

____

____

____

____

____

Monthly Maintenance Check   Year:________

	January	February	March	April	May	June	July	August	September	October	November	December
Battery												
Brakes/Fluid												
Spokes/Wheels												
Sprockets												
Fuel Filter												
Oil Level												
Chassis												
Coolant Level												
Air Filter												
Kickstand												
Hosepipe												
Lights												
Mileage												

Additional Notes:________________________________

____
____
____
____
____
____
____

Monthly Maintenance Check   Year:_________

	January	February	March	April	May	June	July	August	September	October	November	December
Battery												
Brakes/Fluid												
Spokes/Wheels												
Sprockets												
Fuel Filter												
Oil Level												
Chassis												
Coolant Level												
Air Filter												
Kickstand												
Hosepipe												
Lights												
Mileage												

Additional Notes:_______________________________________

____
____
____
____
____
____
____

Monthly Maintenance Check   Year:____________

	January	February	March	April	May	June	July	August	September	October	November	December
Battery												
Brakes/Fluid												
Spokes/Wheels												
Sprockets												
Fuel Filter												
Oil Level												
Chassis												
Coolant Level												
Air Filter												
Kickstand												
Hosepipe												
Lights												
Mileage												

Additional Notes:_______________________________________

____
____
____
____
____
____
____

Monthly Maintenance Check   Year:________

	January	February	March	April	May	June	July	August	September	October	November	December
Battery												
Brakes/Fluid												
Spokes/Wheels												
Sprockets												
Fuel Filter												
Oil Level												
Chassis												
Coolant Level												
Air Filter												
Kickstand												
Hosepipe												
Lights												
Mileage												

Additional Notes:_______________________________________

____
____
____
____
____
____
____

Monthly Maintenance Check   Year: __________

	January	February	March	April	May	June	July	August	September	October	November	December
Battery												
Brakes/Fluid												
Spokes/Wheels												
Sprockets												
Fuel Filter												
Oil Level												
Chassis												
Coolant Level												
Air Filter												
Kickstand												
Hosepipe												
Lights												
Mileage												

Additional Notes: ____

____

____

____

____

____

____

____

Monthly Maintenance Check   Year:________

	January	February	March	April	May	June	July	August	September	October	November	December
Battery												
Brakes/Fluid												
Spokes/Wheels												
Sprockets												
Fuel Filter												
Oil Level												
Chassis												
Coolant Level												
Air Filter												
Kickstand												
Hosepipe												
Lights												
Mileage												

Additional Notes:____________________________________

____

____

____

____

____

____

____

Monthly Maintenance Check   Year: _________

	January	February	March	April	May	June	July	August	September	October	November	December
Battery												
Brakes/Fluid												
Spokes/Wheels												
Sprockets												
Fuel Filter												
Oil Level												
Chassis												
Coolant Level												
Air Filter												
Kickstand												
Hosepipe												
Lights												
Mileage												

Additional Notes: ____

____
____
____
____
____
____
____

Monthly Maintenance Check   Year:_________

	January	February	March	April	May	June	July	August	September	October	November	December
Battery												
Brakes/Fluid												
Spokes/Wheels												
Sprockets												
Fuel Filter												
Oil Level												
Chassis												
Coolant Level												
Air Filter												
Kickstand												
Hosepipe												
Lights												
Mileage												

Additional Notes:_________________________________

____
____
____
____
____
____
____

Monthly Maintenance Check   Year:_________

	January	February	March	April	May	June	July	August	September	October	November	December
Battery												
Brakes/Fluid												
Spokes/Wheels												
Sprockets												
Fuel Filter												
Oil Level												
Chassis												
Coolant Level												
Air Filter												
Kickstand												
Hosepipe												
Lights												
Mileage												

Additional Notes:_________________________________

____

____

____

____

____

____